Collins

Flags of the World

Published by Collins
An imprint of HarperCollins Publishers
1 Robroyston Gate, Glasgow G33 1JN

www.collins.co.uk

HarperCollins Publishers
Macken House, 39/40 Mayor Street, Upper Dublin 1, Ireland D01 C9W8

First published 2024

© HarperCollins Publishers 2024

Collins® is a registered trademark of HarperCollins Publishers Ltd

Text © HarperCollins Publishers 2024

Commissioning Editor: Beth Ralston
Head of Creative Services: Craig Balfour
Art Director: Kevin Robbins
Editorial: Elizabeth Donald, Julianna Dunn, Karen Marland, David Mumford and Lauren Reid

All rights reserved. No part of this publication may be reproduced, stored in a retrieval system, or transmitted, in any form or by any means, electronic, mechanical, photocopying, recording or otherwise without the prior permission in writing of the publisher and copyright owners.

Without limiting the author's and publisher's exclusive rights, any unauthorised use of this publication to train generative artificial intelligence (AI) technologies is expressly prohibited. HarperCollins also exercise their rights under Article 4(3) of the Digital Single Market Directive 2019/790 and expressly reserve this publication from the text and data mining exception.

The contents of this publication are believed correct at the time of printing. Nevertheless the publisher can accept no responsibility for errors or omissions, changes in the detail given or for any expense or loss thereby caused.

A catalogue record for this book is available from the British Library.

ISBN 978-0-00-866351-3

Printed in India

10 9 8 7 6 5 4 3

Collins

Flags of the World

FUN FLAG FACTS, STATS & QUIZZES

CONTENTS

▷▷▷ Introduction 6

? How to use this book .. 7

Country flags 8

Other flags 204

✓ Quizzes 211

Answers 224

Introduction

Are you ready to set off around the world and explore the fascinating world of flags?

Flags come in all colours, shapes and sizes; each with its own unique history, symbolism and story.

Discover flags that have been used for hundreds of years, flags with mysterious symbols and hidden meanings, flags with amazing animals and mythical creatures, and lots more.

Every flag is special, let's find out why...

How to use this book

Afghanistan

Asia   Kabul   41 million   652,225 sq. km

In the last 100 years, Afghanistan has changed its flag more than any other country. It has used 19 different national flags.

Albania

Europe   Tirana   2.8 million   28,748 sq. km

This dramatic flag dates back to the 15th century. The double-headed eagle was used by the army of 'Skanderbeg', a national hero who fought for independence against the Ottoman Empire.

Algeria

 Africa
 Algiers
 45 million
 2,381,741 sq. km

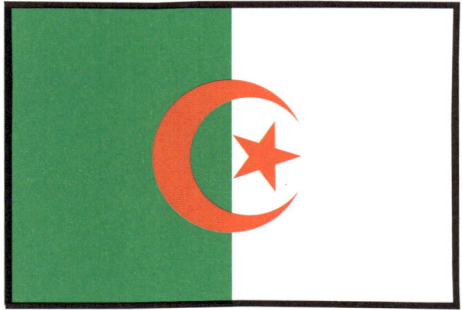

The crescent moon and star in the centre of the Algerian flag represent Islam. The tips of the crescent are longer compared to other countries with a similar design and are said to represent happiness and good luck.

Andorra

Europe   Andorra la Vella   80 thousand   465 sq. km

Andorra is a small country between France and Spain. Unusually, it is ruled by two co-princes, and each of their coat of arms (colourful shields that represent different people or families) appears in the centre of this flag.

Angola

Africa   Luanda   36 million   1,246,700 sq. km

Angola adopted (started using) this flag when it celebrated independence from Portugal in 1975. The yellow cog and machete (a large knife used to cut crops) represent the nation's farming industry.

Antigua and Barbuda

North America

St John's

94 thousand

442 sq. km

Sir Reginald Samuel beat over 600 people in a competition to design this Caribbean country's flag. The seven points on the sun represent the six districts (known as parishes) of Antigua and the island of Barbuda.

Argentina

South America | Buenos Aires | 46 million | 2,766,889 sq. km

A flag like this with three stripes is known as a 'triband'. The sun emblem (a type of symbol used on flags) is called the 'Sun of May' and represents the Incan sun god. It also appears on the Uruguay flag.

Armenia

Asia　　　Yerevan　　　2.8 million　　　29,800 sq. km

The colour of the bottom stripe of Armenia's flag is officially called 'apricot'. The flag has its own national day every year on 15 June.

Australia

Oceania Canberra 26 million 7,692,024 sq. km

Australia is one of four countries, other than the United Kingdom, to feature a Union Jack on its flag. The others are Fiji, New Zealand and Tuvalu.

Austria

Europe   Vienna   8.9 million   83,855 sq. km

This version of the Austrian flag was adopted in 1945, but the red and white bands have been used as a national symbol since 1230. Along with Denmark's flag, it is one of the world's oldest.

Azerbaijan

Asia Baku 10 million 86,600 sq. km

In 2007, this flag was hoisted (raised) up the world's tallest flagpole. The pole stood 162 m tall. The special flag flown was 35 m high, 70 m wide and weighed 350 kg.

Bahrain

Asia   Manama   1.5 million   691 sq. km

Only two country flags contain zigzags between the colours: Bahrain's and Qatar's. The two are often mixed up, but can be told apart by the colour and the number of points on the jagged line.

Bangladesh

Asia

Dhaka

171 million

143,998 sq. km

With a large, red sun-like circle on a plain field, this flag is similar to Japan's design. However, Bangladesh's flag has a green background, not white, and the sun is slightly off-centre to the left.

Barbados

North America

Bridgetown

282 thousand

430 sq. km

The trident (a spear with three prongs) of Poseidon, Greek god of the sea, is a fitting symbol for this island nation. The flag was designed by an art teacher, Grantley W. Prescod, and he stitched the very first flag together himself.

Belarus

Europe   Minsk   9.5 million   207,600 sq. km

The pattern on this flag is traditionally woven into clothing in Belarus. It also appears on decorative cloths used for ceremonies and special events.

Belgium

Europe   **Brussels**   **12 million**   **30,520 sq. km**

The black, yellow and red colours are taken from the Duke of Brabant's coat of arms, which has been around since the 12th century. The area of Brabant is now split between Belgium and the Netherlands.

Belize

North America

Belmopan

405 thousand

22,965 sq. km

No other national flag has large drawings of people on it, although some flags show human hands and other parts of the body. The flag of Belize also uses no fewer than 19 different colours.

Benin

Africa   Porto-Novo   13 million   112,620 sq. km

Benin's flag was first used as the flag of the Republic of Dahomey, which was the name of the country from 1959–1975. A different flag was used from 1975–1990 before this design was used again.

Bhutan

Asia   Thimphu   782 thousand   46,620 sq. km

The beautiful dragon features on this flag because Bhutan is known as the 'Dragon Kingdom' in the local Dzongkha language.

Bolivia

South America | La Paz/Sucre | 12 million | 1,098,581 sq. km

The coat of arms in the middle of this tricolour flag (a flag with three blocks of different colours) has many interesting details, including two animals – a llama and an Andean condor.

Bosnia and Herzegovina

Europe   Sarajevo   3.2 million   51,130 sq. km

This unusual design includes a right-angled triangle, with each point of the triangle representing the Bosniak, Croat and Serb peoples. The stars are meant to look like they are infinite in number, so they run off the top and bottom of the flag.

Botswana

Africa   Gaborone   2.6 million   581,370 sq. km

Botswana's flag is rare in Africa because it doesn't have any yellow, red or green. The light blue represents water, which is very precious in a country that is largely covered by the Kalahari desert.

Brazil

 South America

 Brasília

 215 million

 8,514,879 sq. km

Talk about eye-catching! Brazil's flag features a blue disc of a starry night sky on a yellow rhombus over a green background. The words on the disc mean 'Order and Progress'.

Brunei

Asia | Bandar Seri Begawan | 449 thousand | 5,765 sq. km

Yellow is the traditional colour of royalty in Southeast Asia and here it represents the Sultan of Brunei. The writing on the emblem is in Arabic and reads: 'Always render service with God's guidance'.

Bulgaria

Europe Sofia 6.8 million 110,994 sq. km

From 1947 to 1990 the Bulgarian flag had the national coat of arms in the white band. You can sometimes see this historic version of the Bulgarian flag flown today.

Burkina Faso

Africa   Ouagadougou   23 million   274,200 sq. km

This is one of many African national flags that uses green, yellow and red, known as the Pan-African colours, inspired by the traditional Ethiopian flag.

Burundi

Africa   Gitega   13 million   27,835 sq. km

The three six-pointed stars of red with green borders represent Burundi's national motto: 'Unity, Work, Progress'.

Cambodia

Asia Phnom Penh 17 million 181,035 sq. km

This flag features Angkor Wat, a Hindu-Buddhist temple built in the 12th century. It is the largest religious structure in the world, covering over 1.6 square kilometres.

Cameroon

 Africa
 Yaoundé
 28 million
 475,442 sq. km

Cameroon uses the Pan-African colours of green, red and yellow on its flag. The green stands for lush vegetation, the yellow represents savannah and the red symbolises the country's unity.

Canada

North America   Ottawa   38 million   9,984,670 sq. km

The famous maple leaf design replaced the Union Jack of the United Kingdom as Canada's national flag in 1965. The leaf has 11 points.

Cape Verde

Africa   Praia   593 thousand   4,033 sq. km

This flag features one yellow star for each of the ten main islands of the nation. Nobody lived on the islands until the Portuguese discovered them in the 15th century.

Central African Republic

Africa

Bangui

5.6 million

622,436 sq. km

The country's first president, Barthélemy Boganda, designed this flag. The red band unites the blue and white colours of France (which used to rule the country), with the green and yellow that represent the newly independent republic.

Chad

 Africa
 N'Djaména
 18 million
 1,284,000 sq. km

Chad's flag is now almost identical to Romania's. However, when Chad adopted its flag, the Romanian one was different and had the country's emblem in the middle.

Chile

South America | Santiago/ Valparaíso | 20 million | 756,945 sq. km

In Spanish, this flag is known as *La Estrella Solitaria* – 'The Lone Star'. It is similar to the flag of the US state of Texas, which is known as the 'Lone Star State'.

China

Asia   Beijing   1.4 billion   9,606,802 sq. km

The 'Five-star Red Flag' was designed by Zeng Liansong, a university lecturer. His design originally included a hammer and sickle (a farming tool) in the large star but these were removed to make the flag unique.

Colombia

South America

Bogotá

52 million

1,141,748 sq. km

Unusually for a tricolour design, the bands on Colombia's flag are not evenly sized. The yellow stripe takes up half the flag and the blue and red stripes take a quarter each.

Comoros

Africa   Moroni   837 thousand   1,862 sq. km

The Comoros flag is the eighth different design used by the country in 60 years. Comoros is a group of islands to the east of Africa and is the only Arab nation that is entirely in the southern hemisphere.

Congo

Africa   Brazzaville   6 million   342,000 sq. km

This design was Congo's first flag as an independent nation, but it only lasted ten years before the government changed the design. In 1991, this original yellow-stripe version started to be used again.

Costa Rica

North America

San José

5.2 million

51,100 sq. km

The Costa Rica flag follows a design suggested by Pacífica Fernández Oreamuno, whose husband José María Castro Madriz was the first president of the country.

Côte d'Ivoire

Africa   **Yamoussoukro**   **28 million**   **322,463 sq. km**

This flag is very similar to Ireland's, but with the colour order reversed. The orange band appears at the hoist side (nearest the flagpole) while the green band is at the fly side (the outer side of the flag).

Croatia

Europe Zagreb 4 million 56,538 sq. km

Although this flag uses similar colours in the same order as the Netherlands flag, its coat of arms sets it apart. The checked design is known in Croatian as the 'chessboard'.

Cuba

North America | Havana | 11 million | 110,860 sq. km

This flag was designed in 1849, 53 years before it was officially adopted. It was first used by people who were fighting against the Spanish rulers.

Cyprus

Asia   Nicosia   1.3 million   9,251 sq. km

Cyprus is one of only two nations to feature a map of the country on its flag. The other is Kosovo. The map of Cyprus is a copper colour because the island contains lots of this metal.

Czechia

Europe	Prague	10 million	78,864 sq. km

The country of Czechoslovakia split into two countries in 1992: Czechia and Slovakia. Czechia kept the flag of the old joint country while Slovakia adopted a new one.

Democratic Republic of the Congo

 Africa

 Kinshasa

 99 million

 2,345,410 sq. km

The red diagonal stripe across this flag is described as 'fimbriated', which means it is edged with thinner stripes of a different colour. Only four other country flags have stripes like this.

Denmark

Europe   Copenhagen   5.9 million   43,075 sq. km

The Danish flag is the oldest national flag in continual use. Legend says it was used at the Battle of Lindanise in 1219, and it has certainly been used to represent Denmark since 1625.

Djibouti

Africa Djibouti 1.1 million 23,200 sq. km

Before it was accepted as the national flag, this represented a political party that helped Djibouti gain its independence from France.

Dominica

North America | Roseau | 73 thousand | 750 sq. km

Thanks to the feathers of the Sisserou parrot, this is one of only three national flags to feature the colour purple. The other two are El Salvador and Nicaragua.

Dominican Republic

North America | Santo Domingo | 11 million | 48,442 sq. km

In the coat of arms is a Bible opened at a particular page – John 8: 31-32, which ends with the words 'the truth will set you free'.

East Timor

Asia   Dili   1.3 million   14,874 sq. km

Flags are considered sacred (holy) objects in East Timor. One tip of the star should always point to the top left corner of the flag, but often flags are made with the star pointing straight up.

Ecuador

South America | Quito | 18 million | 272,045 sq. km

Ecuador takes its name from the Spanish for 'equator', because the Equator passes through the northern part of the country. The country's highest mountain, Chimborazo, appears on the flag's shield.

Egypt

Africa   Cairo   110 million   1,001,450 sq. km

The red, white and black tricolour design of Egypt's flag is also used by Iraq, Sudan, Syria and Yemen. The emblem in the white band is Egypt's national symbol, the 'Eagle of Saladin'.

El Salvador

North America

San Salvador

6.3 million

21,041 sq. km

This is one of only five national flags that shows an image of the flag within the flag itself. The other flags that do this belong to Bolivia, the Dominican Republic, Ecuador and Haiti.

Equatorial Guinea

Africa   Malabo   1.7 million   28,051 sq. km

The emblem on this flag features a silk cotton tree. There are six stars, one each for Equatorial Guinea's mainland area and its five main islands.

Eritrea

Africa　　Asmara　　3.7 million　　117,400 sq. km

Three triangles make up Eritrea's flag. The flag's wreath has 30 leaves – one for every year of the country's war for independence from Ethiopia.

Estonia

 Europe   Tallinn    1.3 million    45,200 sq. km

Before it was adopted as the national flag, this was the flag of an Estonian university student society.

Eswatini

Africa Lobamba/Mbabane 1.2 million 17,364 sq. km

Eswatini used to be known as Swaziland. The flag features two spears and a traditional Nguni shield.

Ethiopia

Africa   Addis Ababa   123 million   1,133,880 sq. km

The yellow star-shaped emblem in the middle of Ethiopia's flag is known as a 'pentagram' (a five-pointed star). The lines around it represent rays of light.

Federated States of Micronesia

Oceania Palikir 114 thousand 701 sq. km

With such an ocean-blue flag, it's no surprise that Micronesia is an island nation. It has a total of 607 islands. The flag has four stars, one for each of the country's states.

Fiji

 Oceania　　 Suva　　 930 thousand　　 18,330 sq. km

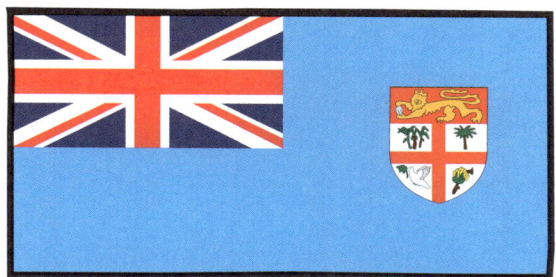

The Prime Minister of Fiji wanted to change the country's flag, but its popularity soared after Fiji won its first-ever Olympic gold medal in Rio de Janeiro in 2016, and the idea was dropped.

Finland

Europe   Helsinki   5.5 million   338,145 sq. km

A cross shifted to the left of a flag is known as a 'Nordic cross'. The Nordic countries of Denmark, Finland, Iceland, Norway and Sweden all have a cross like this on their flag.

France

Europe   Paris   65 million   543,965 sq. km

This design was adopted after the French Revolution. Fighters from Paris wore blue and red rosettes on their hats during the storming of the Bastille in 1789, and white was a traditional colour on French flags.

Gabon

 Africa
 Libreville
 2.4 million
 267,667 sq. km

The Gabon flag is a horizontal tricolour. The colours used in the design represent the country's large areas of forest (green), the Equator (yellow) and long coastline (blue).

Georgia

Asia

Tbilisi

3.7 million

69,700 sq. km

Known as the 'Five-Cross' flag, a similar design first appeared on the war banner of the medieval Kingdom of Georgia in the 12th century.

Germany

Europe　　Berlin　　83 million　　357,022 sq. km

Between 1919 and 1933, the black, red and gold flag of Germany had a height-to-width ratio of 2:3. When it was once again adopted as the national flag in 1949, it was made slightly longer, in a 3:5 ratio.

Ghana

Africa   Accra   33 million   238,537 sq. km

Ghana's flag was designed by Theodosia Okoh, an artist and teacher, shortly after the country became independent. The star in the middle is known as the 'Black Star of Africa'.

Greece

Europe   Athens   10 million   131,957 sq. km

The cross is a Christian symbol, while the blue and white represent the colours of the sea and sky. Legend says there is one stripe for each of the nine syllables in the Greek phrase *Eleftheria i Thanatos*, which means 'Freedom or Death'.

Grenada

North America   St George's   125 thousand   378 sq. km

The emblem on the left-hand green triangle of this flag is a nutmeg. Grenada is one of the world's biggest nutmeg producers and is sometimes called 'Spice Island'.

Guatemala

North America | Guatemala City | 18 million | 108,890 sq. km

The long-tailed bird on the Guatemalan flag is the wonderfully named 'resplendent quetzal'. The quetzal lives in the country's cloud forests and symbolises freedom.

Guinea

Africa   Conakry   14 million   245,857 sq. km

The colours are the same as those on the Ghana flag, but the stripes on Guinea's tricolour are vertical rather than horizontal.

Guinea-Bissau

Africa   Bissau   2.1 million   36,125 sq. km

Several African countries use red, yellow, green and black on their flag. When Guinea-Bissau became independent from Portugal, it took inspiration for its new flag from the flag of Ghana.

Guyana

 South America
 Georgetown
 809 thousand
 214,969 sq. km

Guyana's flag was designed by the American flag expert Whitney Smith. He created the word 'vexillology', which means the study of flags.

Haiti

North America

Port-au-Prince

12 million

27,750 sq. km

In the centre of this flag is Haiti's coat of arms. This features a green lawn with several items on it: a palm tree, cannons, a drum, bugles (small trumpets), anchors and six examples of this very flag.

Honduras

North America   Tegucigalpa   10 million   112,088 sq. km

Honduras has coasts on both the Pacific Ocean and the Caribbean Sea. The two blue bands represent these great bodies of water.

Hungary

 Europe Budapest  10 million  93,030 sq. km

Take care when spotting this flag. Its colours are the same as on Italy's flag, but Hungary's design has horizontal stripes instead of vertical ones.

Iceland

Europe   Reykjavík   373 thousand   102,820 sq. km

Red on flags often represents the blood of fallen heroes, but to Icelanders it stands for the fire that pours from the island's many volcanoes.

India

Asia

New Delhi

1.4 billion

3,166,620 sq. km

India's flag is known as the *Tiraṅgā*, which means 'tricolour'. In the middle is the 'Ashoka Chakra', a 24-spoke wheel symbol used in the Hindu, Jain and Buddhist religions.

Indonesia

Asia   Jakarta   276 million   1,919,445 sq. km

This simple design has flown in Indonesia since it gained independence in 1945, but the use of red and white bands as a banner for the region dates back to the 13th-century Majapahit Empire.

Iran

Asia · Tehran · 89 million · 1,648,000 sq. km

The white script along the edges of the green and red stripes is an Arabic expression called the 'Takbir'. It means 'God is greater' and is written 11 times in each stripe.

Iraq

Asia Baghdad 45 million 438,317 sq. km

The Iraqi flag was a simple tricolour design when it was first adopted. The Takbir script was added in 1991.

Ireland

Europe Dublin 5 million 70,282 sq. km

This flag is a hopeful symbol of peace. The white band in the centre joins together the colours of the country's two main religious groups – green for Roman Catholics and orange for Protestants.

Israel

Asia   Jerusalem*   9 million   22,072 sq. km

At the heart of the Israeli flag is the Star of David, a symbol of Judaism. The shape is a hexagram that can be made from two equilateral triangles.

* disputed capital

Italy

Europe   Rome   59 million   301,245 sq. km

Inspired by the French flag, but redesigned with Italian national colours, this flag is known as *il Tricolore* – 'the Tricolour'.

Jamaica

North America | Kingston | 2.8 million | 10,991 sq. km

Jamaica is the only country in the world not to feature any blue, white or red in its flag.

Japan

Asia   Tokyo   124 million   377,727 sq. km

Japan's nickname is the 'Land of the Rising Sun' and this flag perfectly suits it. Legend says that Japan's Emperor is a direct descendant of the sun goddess Amaterasu.

Jordan

 Asia

 Amman

 11 million

 89,206 sq. km

This is one of seven national flags of Arab nations to feature all of the Pan-Arab colours of black, white, green and red. Other countries that use these colours are Iraq, Kuwait, Libya, Sudan, Syria and United Arab Emirates.

Kazakhstan

Asia   Astana   19 million   2,717,300 sq. km

The soaring eagle beneath a shining sun, the turquoise sky and the golden 'horns of the ram' pattern are the perfect symbols for freedom in the flag of Kazakhstan.

Kenya

 Africa
 Nairobi
 54 million
 582,646 sq. km

The emblem is a traditional shield of the Maasai people (a native Kenyan tribe) laid across two spears.

Kiribati

Oceania   Ambo, Tarawa   131 thousand   717 sq. km

The golden bird on this eye-catching flag is a frigate bird. The sun image has 17 rays – one for each of the populated islands that make up Kiribati.

KOSOVO

Europe **Pristina** **1.7 million** **10,908 sq. km**

Above a golden map of Kosovo are six stars, one for each of the country's biggest ethnic groups: Albanians, Serbs, Bosniaks, Turks, Romani and Gorani.

Kuwait

Asia   Kuwait City   4.3 million   17,818 sq. km

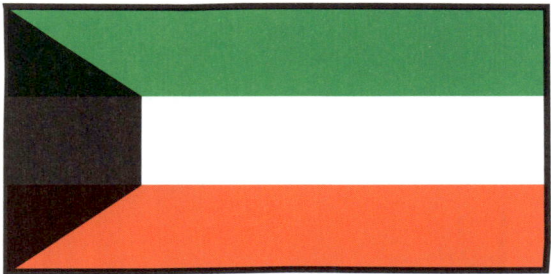

The Kuwait flag was the design on the world's largest-ever kite. The kite had an area of 1,019 square metres and first flew in 2004.

Kyrgyzstan

Asia   Bishkek   6.6 million   198,500 sq. km

Imagine waking up in a yurt – a traditional tent of Asian travellers – and seeing the sun shining in through the hole at the top where the tent poles meet. That's what this flag represents.

Laos

Asia   Vientiane   7.5 million   236,800 sq. km

The current flag of Laos replaced a version that featured a three-headed white elephant under a parasol (an umbrella that protects you from the sun).

Latvia

Europe   Riga   1.9 million   64,589 sq. km

The Latvian flag dates back to the 13th century. It is thought to have been first used by a tribe during a battle for the town of Riga.

Lebanon

Asia   Beirut   5.5 million   10,452 sq. km

The tree on this flag is called the 'cedar of Lebanon', which is the symbol of the country. The cedar of Lebanon is mentioned 77 times in the Bible.

Lesotho

 Africa
 Maseru
 2.3 million
 30,355 sq. km

The emblem in the middle of Lesotho's flag is a 'mokorotlo', a traditional straw hat. Lesotho is a landlocked country that is completely surrounded by South Africa.

Liberia

Africa Monrovia 5.3 million 111,369 sq. km

The flag has 11 stripes – one for each person who signed Liberia's Declaration of Independence.

Libya

Africa Tripoli 6.8 million 1,759,540 sq. km

The crescent moon symbolises the start of the lunar month according to the Muslim calendar and the beginning of the Prophet Muhammad's journey from Mecca.

Liechtenstein

Europe Vaduz 39 thousand 160 sq. km

Liechtenstein added a gold crown to its flag in 1937 after realising the blue and red design was the same as Haiti's.

Lithuania

Europe   Vilnius   2.8 million   65,200 sq. km

When Lithuania was part of the Soviet Union, its flag featured a hammer and sickle emblem. Lithuania has been independent since 1990 and the old Soviet flag has been outlawed since 2008.

Luxembourg

Europe

Luxembourg

648 thousand

2,586 sq. km

A law says that this flag must be made with a very bright blue and red to tell it apart from the Netherlands flag, which has the same basic design. Luxembourg's flag is also a little wider.

Madagascar

Africa   Antananarivo   30 million   587,041 sq. km

Madagascar adopted its new national flag two years before it actually became independent from France.

Malawi

 Africa
 Lilongwe
 20 million
 118,484 sq. km

The rising sun emblem has 31 rays to show that Malawi was the 31st African nation when it became independent.

Malaysia

Asia   Kuala Lumpur/   34 million   332,965
         Putrajaya   sq. km

In Malay, this flag is called *Jalur Gemilang* or 'Stripes of Glory'. The flag is in two flag families (flags with similar designs): the Muslim crescent, and the stars and stripes.

Maldives

 Asia

 Male

 524 thousand

 298 sq. km

The crescent moon is a symbol on the flags of many Islamic nations. The island chain of the Maldives lies in the Indian Ocean and its official religion is Sunni Islam.

Mali

Africa   Bamako   23 million   1,240,140 sq. km

The flag of Mali features the same colours as the flag of Guinea, but with the colours in the opposite order.

Malta

Europe   **Valletta**   533 thousand   316 sq. km

The George Cross that features on the top left of the Malta flag was given to the island for their heroism during WWII. Malta is the only country with a military award on its flag.

Marshall Islands

Oceania | Delap-Uliga-Djarrit, Majuro | 42 thousand | 181 sq. km

This flag was designed by Emlain Kabua, an artist and the First Lady of the Marshall Islands when the nation became independent.

Mauritania

Africa   Nouakchott   4.7 million   1,030,700 sq. km

This is one of the world's youngest flags. It was adopted in 2017 after the Mauritanian people voted for a new flag in a referendum.

Mauritius

Africa   Port Louis   1.3 million   2,040 sq. km

Each of the colours in this flag means something special: red represents the struggle for independence; blue symbolises the Indian Ocean; yellow represents the country's bright future; and green symbolises farming.

Mexico

North America   Mexico City   128 million   1,972,545 sq. km

The coat of arms in the centre is based on the Aztec symbol for Tenochtitlan, the capital city of the Aztec Empire in the 15th century. Mexico City stands on the ruins of this ancient settlement.

Moldova

Europe

Chisinau

3.3 million

33,700 sq. km

The only difference between Moldova's flag and that of its neighbour, Romania, is that Moldova's features the country's coat of arms – an eagle and shield with the head of an aurochs (extinct cattle) on it.

Monaco

Europe   Monaco-Ville   36 thousand   2 sq. km

Is this Monaco's flag or Indonesia's? They are both half red, half white with the red half on top. And if you flip this design upside down, you have the flag of Poland – white on top of red.

Mongolia

 Asia   Ulan Bator    3.4 million    1,565,000 sq. km

On the left of this flag, the yellow 'Soyombo' is a national symbol of Mongolia. The red bands represent progress and freedom; the blue band symbolises open blue sky.

Montenegro

Europe   Podgorica   627 thousand   13,812 sq. km

The golden eagle on this flag's coat of arms is crowned and carries two important symbols in its talons – a sceptre (the stick) and an orb with a cross on top (the circular object).

Morocco

Africa   Rabat   37 million   446,550 sq. km

The green pentagram is a symbol of the Seal of Solomon. The ancient King of Morocco wore the symbol on a ring that was said to have given him the power to talk with animals.

Mozambique

Africa Maputo 33 million 799,380 sq. km

There are four countries that have guns on their flag, but Mozambique is the only one to have a modern weapon. The flags of Bolivia, Guatemala and Haiti feature cannons or rifles.

Myanmar

Asia   Nay Pyi Taw   54 million   676,577 sq. km

When this flag was adopted in 2010, the Myanmar government ordered that all old national flags should be burned. The country is also known as Burma.

Namibia

Africa　　Windhoek　　2.6 million　　824,292 sq. km

When Namibia became independent from South Africa it held a competition to design a new flag. Out of the 870 entries, the three best designs were combined to create the new flag.

Nauru

Oceania — Yaren — 13 thousand — 21 sq. km

Part map, part flag – Nauru's design celebrates the island's location. The yellow line is the Equator and the star represents the island itself, close to the Equator in the blue Pacific Ocean.

Nepal

Asia   Kathmandu   31 million   147,181 sq. km

This is the only national flag in the world that is not a rectangle or a square. The design is made of two pennants (triangular flags) merged together. The emblems represent the moon and the sun.

Netherlands

Europe   Amsterdam/   18 million   41,526
           The Hague   sq. km

The Dutch flag is the oldest tricolour flag still in use today. This design inspired the French and Russian flags and many other tricolours.

New Zealand

Oceania   Wellington   5.2 million   270,534 sq. km

The Union Jack appears in what is known as a 'canton' – a rectangle on the hoist side, nearest the flagpole. The stars represent the Southern Cross constellation.

Nicaragua

North America

Managua

6.9 million

130,000 sq. km

The coat of arms in the centre of this flag features five volcanoes, as well as a rising sun, a rainbow to symbolise peace and a red cap to represent liberty.

Niger

Africa   Niamey   26 million   1,267,000 sq. km

The circle emblem in the middle of the flag is known as a 'roundel'. For Niger it represents the warm sun and the independence of the nation.

Nigeria

Africa Abuja 219 million 923,768 sq. km

Michael Taiwo Akinkunmi was a student living in London when he designed Nigeria's flag. He is known in his community as 'Mr Flag Man'.

North Korea

Asia Pyongyang 26 million 120,538 sq. km

North Korea flies a huge national flag from the world's fourth-tallest flagpole. The pole is 160 m high and the flag weighs 270 kg.

North Macedonia

Europe

Skopje

2.1 million

25,713 sq. km

A comic artist and architect called Miroslav Grčev created the North Macedonian flag.

Norway

Europe   Oslo   5.4 million   323,878 sq. km

The law states that you must fold Norway's flag in a certain way when you take it down, and must never let it touch the ground. It is also never to be worn below the waist.

Oman

Asia   Muscat   4.6 million   309,500 sq. km

Oman's national symbol is on the vertical red stripe of its flag. It shows a J-shaped khanjar dagger, laid over two crossed swords.

Pakistan

Asia　　Islamabad　　236 million　　881,888 sq. km

Pakistan's flag is sung about in the country's national anthem as an 'inspiration for our future'.

Palau

Asia　　　Ngerulmud　　18 thousand　　497 sq. km

It may look like the sun, but the yellow disc actually represents the moon, which is a symbol of peace and love in Palau. Sowing seeds, harvesting crops and many celebrations happen at full moon.

Panama

 North America

 Panama City

 4.4 million

 77,082 sq. km

The rules are that this flag must be run up its pole after 7 a.m. and taken down before 6 p.m. Anyone present must take their hat off and place their right hand on their chest in respect.

Papua New Guinea

Oceania — Port Moresby — 10 million — 462,840 sq. km

This flag was designed by 15-year-old schoolgirl Susan Karike and it won a national competition. It shows the Southern Cross constellation and a tropical bird called a 'bird of paradise'.

Paraguay

South America

Asunción

6.8 million

406,752 sq. km

This is one of only three national flags that are different on the front and the back ('obverse' and 'reverse' as they are known by flag experts). The others belong to Moldova and Saudi Arabia.

Peru

South America

Lima

34 million

1,285,216 sq. km

The first design for Peru's flag had a flaming red sun in the middle of the white stripe. This was swapped for the country's coat of arms a few years later. The emblem was removed completely in 1950.

Philippines

Asia | Manila | 116 million | 300,000 sq. km

If the flag of the Philippines is flown upside down with the red band on top, it means that the country is at war.

Poland

Europe   Warsaw   40 million   312,683 sq. km

Poland's flag is one of only five country flags that have a height-to-width ratio of 5:8. The others are Argentina, Guatemala, Palau and Sweden.

Portugal

 Europe
 Lisbon
 10 million
 88,940 sq. km

The golden circular symbol on this flag is something called an 'armillary sphere', a 3D map of the Earth and stars used by sailors in the past. It reflects Portugal's history of exploring the world by sea.

Qatar

Asia Doha 2.7 million 11,437 sq. km

Qatar's zigzag design is similar to its neighbour Bahrain's, although it has nine white points rather than five. It's the only national flag that's more than twice as wide as it is high.

Romania

Europe   Bucharest   20 million   237,500 sq. km

The largest flag ever created was a Romanian flag. It measured 349 m by 227 m, with an area of 79,290 square metres – bigger than nine football pitches. It was displayed in 2013.

Russia

Asia/Europe   Moscow   145 million   17,075,400 sq. km

Russian Tsar Peter the Great ordered a ship from Amsterdam and when it arrived from the shipyard it was flying the Dutch banner. Peter modelled the Russian flag on that banner.

Rwanda

Africa   Kigali   14 million   26,338 sq. km

This design reflects the lush landscape of Rwanda, under the warm light of the sun. The sun has 24 rays.

St Kitts and Nevis

North America

Basseterre

48 thousand

261 sq. km

This flag has a star for each of the country's two islands and was designed by a student called Edrice Lewis. St Kitts and Nevis is the smallest country in the Western Hemisphere.

St Lucia

North America | Castries | 180 thousand | 616 sq. km

The black and white triangles represent the Pitons, St Lucia's twin volcanic peaks. The yellow triangle celebrates the sunshine that this Caribbean island enjoys.

St Vincent and the Grenadines

North America | Kingstown | 104 thousand | 389 sq. km

This Caribbean nation has a main island called St Vincent and a chain of 32 smaller islands called the Grenadines, known as the 'Gems of the Antilles'. The flag is sometimes called 'The Gems'.

Samoa

 Oceania
 Apia
 222 thousand
 2,831 sq. km

This flag features the Southern Cross, a bright constellation visible in Samoa. It is not visible in Europe, North America or most of Asia.

San Marino

Europe | San Marino | 34 thousand | 61 sq. km

San Marino is the fifth-smallest country in the world. The coat of arms on its flag shows three towers on three peaks, a famous symbol of the nation's capital city, which is also called San Marino.

São Tomé and Príncipe

Africa

São Tomé

227 thousand

964 sq. km

This flag was adopted when the islands gained their independence from Portugal. It was designed by the new nation's first president, Manuel Pinto da Costa.

Saudi Arabia

Asia　　　Riyadh　　　36 million　　2,200,000 sq. km

The Arabic script on this flag states 'There is no god but God; Muhammad is the Messenger of God'. As this is holy, the flag design is not allowed on items such as T-shirts or footballs.

Senegal

 Africa
 Dakar
 17 million
 196,720 sq. km

The style of this flag is similar to the French tricolour, which was the flag of Senegal before its independence. However, the new design has colours that are meaningful to the Senegalese people.

Serbia

Europe | Belgrade | 7.2 million | 77,453 sq. km

The silver double-headed eagle on the coat of arms has been a symbol of Serbian royalty since the 11th century.

Seychelles

 Africa
 Victoria
 107 thousand
 455 sq. km

Here's a flag that's a real ray of sunshine! This flag was designed to represent a new dawn for a country that had just gained its independence from the United Kingdom.

Sierra Leone

Africa   Freetown   8.6 million   71,740 sq. km

Sierra Leone's flag was created by the College of Arms in London. The college is an authority on coats of arms, national symbols and flags.

Singapore

Asia   Singapore   6 million   639 sq. km

This flag was first adopted when Singapore became self-governing (able to make its own laws) in 1959. It continued as the nation's flag when it became fully independent from the United Kingdom six years later.

Slovakia

Europe   Bratislava   5.6 million   49,035 sq. km

Slovakia's national flag is one of 28 that feature a Christian symbol. The national coat of arms, with its double cross emblem, is laid on top of a tricolour that is very similar to the Russian flag.

Slovenia

Europe   Ljubljana   2.1 million   20,251 sq. km

The Slovenian flag features the country's coat of arms on a red, white and blue tricolour. The mountain on the emblem is Triglav, the highest mountain in Slovenia at 2,864 m.

Solomon Islands

Oceania　　Honiara　　724 thousand　　28,370 sq. km

The stars stand for the five original districts, known as provinces, of the Solomon Islands. Today there are nine provinces, so perhaps the flag should be updated!

Somalia

 Africa
 Mogadishu
 18 million
 637,657 sq. km

Somalia is on the east coast of Africa and the blue in this flag reflects its ocean-side position and its open skies. The star has five points, one for each of the regions its people live in.

South Africa

 Africa

 Bloemfontein/ Cape Town/Pretoria

 60 million

 1,219,090 sq. km

This flag was adopted during the first election in which all South Africans were able to vote. It was waved during their Rugby World Cup triumph at home a year later in 1995.

South Korea

Asia   Seoul   52 million   99,274 sq. km

The red-and-blue 'Taegeuk' symbol represents balance in the universe. The four sets of black lines represent the elements of earth, air, fire and water, as well as the four points of a compass.

South Sudan

Africa   Juba   11 million   644,329 sq. km

This flag is six years older than the country it represents. The flag was adopted in 2005, but South Sudan did not become independent until 2011.

Spain

 Europe   Madrid    45 million    504,782 sq. km

Spain's flag is known as *la Rojigualda*, which means 'red and yellow'. A yellow stripe joins two red stripes that are half its height.

Sri Lanka

Asia   Sri Jayawardenapura Kotte   22 million   65,610 sq. km

Here's a flag with a distinctive design! The 'Sinha' flag of Sri Lanka features a golden lion holding a traditional kasthane sword in its right front paw.

Sudan

 Africa
 Khartoum
 47 million
 1,861,484 sq. km

Sudan's flag uses the popular Pan-Arab colours. Countries share these colours to show the togetherness of Arab people across national borders.

Suriname

South America

Paramaribo

618 thousand

163,820 sq. km

When Suriname became independent from the Netherlands, a national competition was held to create a new flag. This winning design was entered by an art teacher called Jack Pinas.

Sweden

Europe   **Stockholm**   **11 million**   **449,964 sq. km**

Only four countries have blue-and-yellow flags, the others being Kazakhstan, Palau and Ukraine. Sweden has used these colours since the reign of King Magnus III in 1275.

Switzerland

Europe   Bern   8.7 million   41,293 sq. km

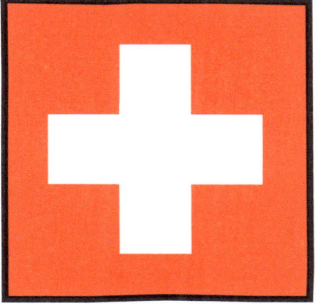

This is one of only two square flags in the world – the other is that of Vatican City. The white cross was used as a symbol by Swiss soldiers as early as the 13th century.

Syria

Asia   Damascus   22 million   184,026 sq. km

This is the official flag of Syria, however, some politicians want to use a different flag that uses a tricolour of green, white and black.

Taiwan

Asia · Taipei · 24 million · 36,179 sq. km

This flag cannot be used at the Olympics as China claims Taiwan to be part of its land. Taiwanese athletes compete under a different flag showing a flower and the Olympic rings.

Tajikistan

Asia | Dushanbe | 10 million | 143,100 sq. km

Tajikistan celebrated 20 years of independence by building a 165-m-tall flagpole in 2011. It was the tallest in the world – but only for three years.

Tanzania

Africa   Dodoma   65 million   945,087 sq. km

This is one of only a few national flags to feature a diagonal band across the design. It was adopted when the states of Tanganyika and Zanzibar were merged to form a single country.

Thailand

Asia   Bangkok   72 million   513,115 sq. km

Legend says that a king of Thailand chose this design because he wanted a flag that looked the same even when it was upside down. The previous flag had an elephant on it.

The Bahamas

North America   Nassau   410 thousand   13,939 sq. km

The golden band represents the warm sunshine, the aquamarine bands are for the waters around the islands and the black triangle represents the strength of the people.

The Gambia

Africa • Banjul • 2.7 million • 11,295 sq. km

The Gambia is named after the Gambia river. It is the smallest country in mainland Africa. When the country became independent from the United Kingdom, its new flag was created by Louis Thomasi, an accountant.

Togo

Africa · Lomé · 8.8 million · 56,785 sq. km

The ratio of a flag's height to its width is often 1:2 or 3:5. Togo's flag is the only one in the world that uses the 'golden ratio' for its dimensions, which is around 1:1.6.

Tonga

 Oceania   Nuku'alofa  107 thousand  748 sq. km

In Tonga, it has been agreed that the national flag design can never be changed. The cross represents Christianity, the religion of 97 per cent of Tongans.

Trinidad and Tobago

North America | Port of Spain | 1.5 million | 5,130 sq. km

Trinidad and Tobago's flag is rare because it features a diagonal line across it, and even rarer because the line goes down towards the right.

Tunisia

Africa   Tunis   12 million   164,150 sq. km

This flag was created by the Bey of Tunis, the monarch of Tunisia. The crescent moon and star are traditional symbols of Islam.

Turkey

Asia/Europe   Ankara   85 million   779,452 sq. km

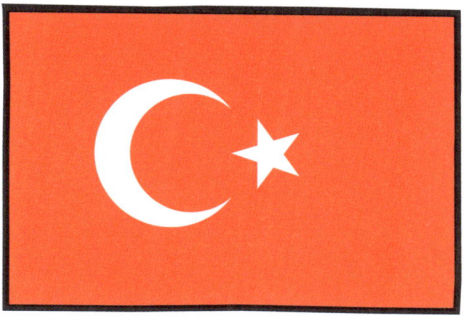

The modern Turkish flag is the same as the last flag of the Ottoman Empire, which ruled large areas of the eastern Mediterranean from the 14th century to the 20th century.

Turkmenistan

 Asia

 Ashgabat

 6.4 million

 488,100 sq. km

Is this the world's most intricate flag? The design celebrates Turkmenistan's historic carpet-weaving industry. There are five carpet designs in the red band, one for each of the country's major tribes.

Tuvalu

Oceania | Vaiaku, Funafuti | 11 thousand | 25 sq. km

The nine stars match the nine islands that make up this nation, though 'Tuvalu' means 'eight together', as originally only eight of the islands were lived on. Tuvalu was once a British dependency.

Uganda

Africa   Kampala   47 million   241,038 sq. km

The grey crowned crane is the national symbol of Uganda and a bird known for its gentle nature. Its leg is raised to symbolise the country stepping forward into the future.

Ukraine

Europe   Kyiv   40 million   603,700 sq. km

This design shows the country's wide wheat fields under a summer sky. The 'Day of the National Flag' is celebrated in Ukraine on 23 August each year.

United Arab Emirates

Asia

Abu Dhabi

9.4 million

77,700 sq. km

This flag was created by Abdullah Mohammed Al Maainah, who was just 19 years old when he designed it.

United Kingdom

Europe

London

68 million

243,609 sq. km

The Union Jack (or Union Flag) is made up of the St George's Cross of England, St Andrew's Cross of Scotland and St Patrick's Cross of Ireland.

United States

North America | Washington, D.C. | 338 million | 9,826,635 sq. km

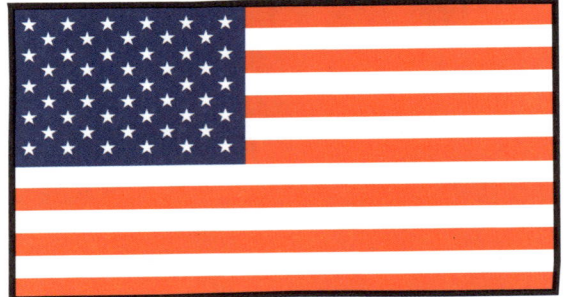

The famous 'Stars and Stripes' is actually the 27th different design since 1777. The 13 stripes mark the colonies that declared independence from Great Britain and there is a star for each of the 50 US states.

Uruguay

South America | Montevideo | 3.4 million | 176,215 sq. km

This flag has a 'Sun of May' emblem with 16 rays – eight straight rays and eight wavy ones. It was designed by Joaquín Suárez, one of Uruguay's first leaders.

Uzbekistan

Asia   Tashkent   35 million   447,400 sq. km

The thin red stripes that contrast the main colours on this flag are known as 'fimbriations'. Uzbekistan was the first Central Asian country to create its own flag after the breakup of the Soviet Union.

Vanuatu

Oceania   Port Vila   327 thousand   12,190 sq. km

Is it a shell? An animal horn? Actually, the golden curl emblem is a boar's tusk. Tusks are a traditional symbol of wealth in Vanuatu and are often worn on necklaces by islanders.

Vatican City

Europe   Vatican City   510   0.5 sq. km

This flag was designed in the same year that Vatican City became independent from Italy, creating the smallest country in the world at just 0.5 square kilometres in area.

Venezuela

 South America

 Caracas

 28 million

 912,050 sq. km

The military leader Francisco de Miranda created the first version of Venezuela's flag. His design also inspired the flags of Colombia and Ecuador.

Vietnam

Asia   Hanoi   98 million   329,565 sq. km

Vietnam's flag is the only one of the ten Southeast Asian countries that does not contain white.

Yemen

 Asia
 Sanaa
 34 million
 527,968 sq. km

This tricolour was adopted when the states of North Yemen and South Yemen united to become a single new country – the Republic of Yemen.

Zambia

Africa   Lusaka   20 million   752,614 sq. km

The bird on the Zambian flag is the African fish eagle. The law states that the flag should only be flown between sunrise and sunset.

Zimbabwe

 Africa
 Harare
16 million
390,759 sq. km

The Zimbabwe bird that features on this flag is the country's national emblem. The design is taken from sculptures found in the ruined medieval city of Great Zimbabwe.

Other flags

Did you know that it's not just countries that have flags? There are lots of different states, territories, dependencies and organisations that have their own flag too. Here are a few from around the world...

Aruba

The star represents the island of Aruba, surrounded by the blue Caribbean Sea. It is coloured red for the love that Arubans have for their island.

Christmas Island

The bird on this flag is a golden bosun, a sea bird native to this tropical island, which is in the Indian Ocean.

Cook Islands

The 15 small islands and atolls that make up this Pacific Island group are each represented by a star on this flag, which was first flown in 1979.

England

The English flag is called the 'St George's Cross' after the patron saint of England. It is said to symbolise his bravery.

Faroe Islands

The Nordic cross and colours on this island group's flag make it similar to the flags of two of its neighbours: Iceland and Norway.

French Polynesia

The coat of arms shows a Polynesian canoe on the sea. The five stars onboard represent the five island groups that make up this Pacific Ocean territory.

Gibraltar

The fortress and key are said to symbolise the idea that Gibraltar holds the key to the Mediterranean Sea, due to its location where the sea meets the Atlantic Ocean.

Greenland

The colours of this flag match Denmark's flag, because Greenland is a territory of Denmark. The circle represents the sun setting on the horizon.

Guernsey

In 1985, William the Conqueror's gold cross was added to the St George's Cross of the English flag to give this island dependency its first official flag.

Hong Kong

Hong Kong's flag, which features a bauhinia flower as a symbol of unity, was adopted in 1997 after the United Kingdom handed this region over to China.

Isle of Man

The symbol of three legs at the centre of this flag is known as a 'triskelion'. It is said to represent the island's three ancient kingdoms.

Jersey

The three lions on this flag's coat of arms are in a walking position with faces turned. This is known as 'lion passant guardant'.

Macao

A lotus flower sits above a stylisation of the region's Governor Nobre de Carvalho Bridge. The white lines represent water, and Macao's history as a port.

Norfolk Island

The tree at the centre of this flag is the native Norfolk Island pine. Green is used in the design to symbolise the island's fertile land and abundant vegetation.

Puerto Rico

This Caribbean island is a territory of the US. Its flag is a variant of the Cuban flag. Both islands were the last two Spanish colonies in the New World.

Scotland

This flag is known as the 'Saltire' and features the white St Andrew's Cross. It has been in use since 1385, making it one of the oldest flags still in use.

Wales

The Welsh flag is called *Y Ddraig Goch*, which means 'the Red Dragon' in Welsh. It represents the triumph of Wales over its enemies in a legendary battle.

European Union

The circles on this flag are a symbol of unity. They symbolise harmony among the countries of Europe.

NATO

The North Atlantic Treaty Organization was formed to promote freedom and democracy for its members. The compass symbolises the direction towards peace.

United Nations

Adopted in 1947, this flag helps the organisation's workers to be recognised in areas of conflict. The blue background and olive branches represent peace.

Quizzes

Are you a quiz whizz?

Test your knowledge in these brain-bending flag quizzes. If you are stuck and need some help, look back over the flag pages for a hint – all of the answers can be found in this book.

Once you've finished a quiz, you can check if your answers are correct on page 224.

Name that flag!

1.
2.
3.
4.
5.
6.
7.
8.

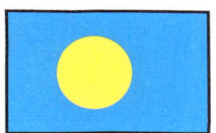   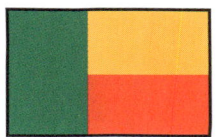

Name that flag... similar but different!

1.
2.

Japan or Bangladesh?

3.
4.

Australia or New Zealand?

5.
6.

India or Niger?

7.
8.

Romania or Chad?

9  10

Colombia or Venezuela?

11  12

Slovenia or Slovakia?

13  14

Netherlands or Luxembourg?

15  16

Poland or Indonesia?

Cool colours

1 If you reversed the colours of the Côte d'Ivoire flag, what country's flag would be made?
   a. Ireland
   b. Iraq
   c. Iran

2 Red and which other colour make up the chessboard design in the flag of Croatia?
   a. Black   b. White   c. Grey

3 Which other European country does Hungary share its flag colours with?
   a. Andorra   b. Latvia   c. Italy

4 What does the red in the Iceland flag represent?
   a. Fire from volcanoes
   b. Sunset
   c. Icelandic flowers

5 Which island country has a copper-coloured map on its national flag?
   a. Samoa   b. Malta   c. Cyprus

6 Which colour is the cedar tree at the centre of the Lebanon flag?

a. Brown   b. Green   c. Black

7 What is the fruity name of the colour at the bottom of the Armenia flag?

a. Apricot
b. Peach
c. Mandarin

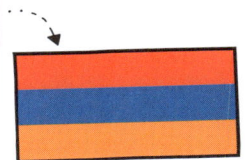

8 Which colour in the Brunei flag represents royalty?

a. Yellow   b. Purple   c. Blue

9 Which is the only country not to have blue, white or red in its flag?

a. Haiti   b. Jamaica   c. Belize

10 What does the yellow in the flag of Ukraine represent?

a. Sandy beaches
b. Gold
c. Wheat

Nifty nicknames

1 What is the nickname given to the flag of the United Kingdom?

a. Union Jack
b. Big Jack
c. Flying Jack

2 Which European country has a flag called *il Tricolore*, meaning 'the Tricolour'?

a. Sweden   b. Italy   c. Estonia

3 Which Asian country's flag is known as the 'Five-star Red Flag'?

a. China   b. Pakistan   c. India

4 Which name is sometimes given to the flag of the United States?

a. Star Flyer
b. Big Apple
c. Stars and Stripes

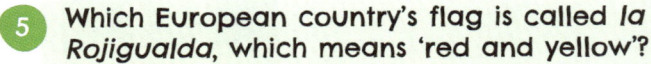

5 Which European country's flag is called *la Rojigualda*, which means 'red and yellow'?

a. Norway   b. Spain   c. Netherlands

6 Which South American country's flag is called 'The Lone Star'?

a. Chile   b. Brazil   c. Paraguay

7 Which nickname was given to the designer of the Nigeria flag?

a. Captain Flag
b. The Flag Doctor
c. Mr Flag Man

8 Which Asian country does the 'Five-Cross' flag belong to?

a. Bhutan   b. Yemen   c. Georgia

9 'Stripes of Glory' is the name given to which Asian country's flag?

a. Mongolia   b. Malaysia   c. Myanmar

10 What is the flag of St Vincent and the Grenadines sometimes called?

a. The Stones
b. The Diamonds
c. The Gems

Dazzling designs

1. Which is the only country in the world not to have a square or rectangular design?
   a. Nepal
   b. Norway
   c. North Macedonia

2. What type of leaf appears at the centre of the Canada flag?
   a. Maple   b. Oak   c. Birch

3. Which item of clothing features on the Lesotho flag?
   a. Gloves   b. Scarf   c. Hat

4. Which Caribbean country's flag contains the trident of Poseidon?
   a. Bahamas
   b. Barbados
   c. Jamaica

5. Which temple is on the Cambodia flag?
   a. Angkor Why   b. Angkor Wat   c. Angkor Who

6 Which African country has a shield of the Maasai people in the cente?

a. Togo   b. Kenya   c. Mali

7 Which spice features on the flag of Grenada?

a. Chilli   b. Nutmeg   c. Pepper

8 Which country in Central America is the only world flag to contain large pictures of people?

a. Belize
b. Panama
c. El Salvador

9 Which mountain features on the flag of Ecuador?

a. Everest   b. Elbrus   c. Chimborazo

10 Which African country has a silk cotton tree in the centre?

a. Equatorial Guinea
b. Somalia
c. Burkina Faso

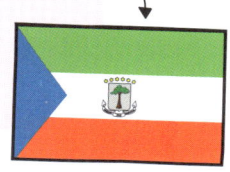

Creature features

1. Which Central American country shows a resplendent quetzal in the centre?

   a. Belize
   b. Honduras
   c. Guatemala

2. Which double-headed bird appears on the flag of Albania?

   a. Eagle   b. Robin   c. Chicken

3. Which animal used to feature on the flag of Thailand?

   a. Elephant   b. Polar bear   c. Tiger

4. Which country has the African fish eagle in its design?

   a. Ghana
   b. Zambia
   c. South Africa

5. Which big cat features on the flag of Sri Lanka?

   a. Jaguar   b. Leopard   c. Lion

6. Which South American country has a llama and an Andean condor in its design?

   a. Peru   b. Brazil   c. Bolivia

7. Which Asian country's flag has a bird of paradise on it?

   a. Papua New Guinea   b. Japan   c. Laos

8. Which country in Oceania has the tusk of a wild boar in its design?

   a. New Zealand
   b. Vanuatu
   c. Tonga

9. Which bird appears at the centre of the Dominica flag?

   a. Penguin   b. Parrot   c. Puffin

10. Which African country features a grey crowned crane at the centre?

   a. Uganda
   b. Nigeria
   c. Morocco

Answers

Name that flag

1. United Kingdom
2. Canada
3. Brazil
4. South Africa
5. Pakistan
6. Jamaica
7. Mexico
8. United Arab Emirates
9. Saudi Arabia
10. Peru
11. North Macedonia
12. Samoa
13. Seychelles
14. Djibouti
15. Palau
16. Benin

Name that flag... similar but different!

1. Japan
2. Bangladesh
3. Australia
4. New Zealand
5. Niger
6. India
7. Chad
8. Romania
9. Venezuela
10. Colombia
11. Slovakia
12. Slovenia
13. Luxembourg
14. Netherlands
15. Poland
16. Indonesia

Cool colours

1. a
2. b
3. c
4. a
5. c
6. b
7. a
8. a
9. b
10. c

Nifty nicknames

1. a
2. b
3. a
4. c
5. b
6. a
7. c
8. c
9. b
10. c

Dazzling designs

1. a
2. a
3. c
4. b
5. b
6. b
7. b
8. a
9. c
10. a

Creature features

1. c
2. a
3. a
4. b
5. c
6. c
7. a
8. b
9. b
10. a